Alcohol: Use, Nonuse and Abuse

D0555926

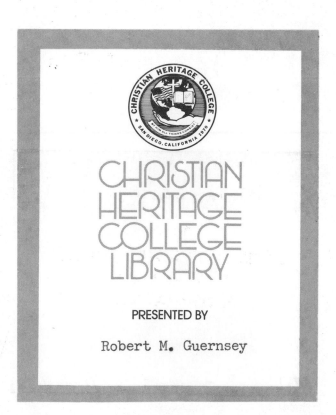

→ Alcohol: Use, Nonuse and Abuse

Charles R. *obert* Carroll
Ball State University, Muncie, Indiana

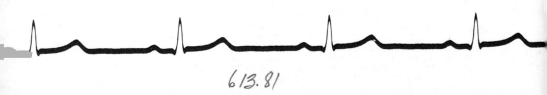

613.81

WM. C. BROWN COMPANY PUBLISHERS
Dubuque, Iowa

CONTEMPORARY TOPICS IN HEALTH SCIENCE SERIES

Consulting Editor
ROBERT KAPLAN
Ohio State University

Copyright ©1970 by Wm. C. Brown Company Publishers

Library of Congress Catalog Card Number: 69—17919

ISBN 0—697—07326—2

Fourth Printing, 1972

Printed in the United States of America

Preface

This text represents an educator's synthesis of facts and comments pertaining to one of the nation's foremost health problems—the use, non-use, and abuse of beverage alcohol. Planned primarily for use in college health science classes, this concise volume can be adapted easily for use in teacher-education programs. Although content is emphasized while methodology is excluded, teachers will be able to use this work as a framework for planning learning experiences appropriate to alcohol education.

The dimensions of the alcohol story have been told many times in a variety of ways. However, this statement of current facts and interpretive remarks highlights some important concepts frequently omitted in the traditional approaches to education about alcohol. Among these concepts are: the use of alcohol is a widespread custom in America's social life; conflict and controversy mark the use of alcohol in this country and generate many alcohol problems; various motivations, together with continuous decision-making, determine the use, non-use, and abuse of alcohol; the body acts upon alcohol and alcohol acts upon the body; and alcoholism is only one form of problem-drinking.

While no suggested activities are offered, there are posed throughout the text several questions which can serve as a basis for class discussion. In addition, numerous authoritative sources are documented in the footnotes and in the selected references. Many of these sources and a wealth of other informative materials about alcohol will be available from public libraries, local health departments, state departments of education and health, and the U.S. Department of Health, Education, and Welfare.

Charles R. Carroll

Foreword

Health education is more than the primary phase of preventive medicine. Beyond the prevention of disease and the amelioration of health problems is its positive design to raise levels of well-being and liberate man's potential. Directly and indirectly it enables the individual to function most productively, creatively, and humanely.

One needs health to become educated and one needs education to develop and maintain health. Nor can one make full use of his education without it. Health is vital to the attainment of goals but we cannot preoccupy ourselves seeking it or in our obsession we shall fail to integrate all aspects of our development and performance. Health is a means to ends—the ends valued by the individual and society. Favorable modifications of health behaviors are essential to the attainment of these ends.

Contemporary Topics in Health Science offers a new and individualized format. Students and instructors can select and utilize those topics most relevant or most pertinent for the time available. Independent and class study, separately or concurrently, are enhanced by their organization. In this form they also provide greater opportunity to correlate health with other subjects.

Each book offers an up-to-date realistic discussion of currently significant health topics. Each explores its area in somewhat greater depth, with less trivia, than found in many textbook chapters. But they are designed to do more than merely present information. Within each are to be found more than partial explanations of facts. They are written by authors ranked by his professional peers as an authority in his field. They encourage the exploration of ideas, development of concepts, identifying value judgements, and selecting from a range of alternatives to enhance critical decision-making.

ROBERT KAPLAN

Contents

CHAPTER 1

Alcohol and American Life

The general topic is alcohol, but in reality the focus is on people—people who use, do not use, and abuse one of the common modifiers of human feeling and behavior.

In this age of uncertainty, change and controversy, many interpretations of basic alcohol facts have been made. The so-called traditional views, expressed in emotion-charged extremes of either "wet" or "dry," still command a considerable following. But the alcohol "new-think" has arrived on the American scene. This new way of thinking about the interrelatedness of human problems dealing with alcohol stands between those extremes of drinking and abstaining. Such a gray zone, which has a potential to generate a coordinated national policy on alcohol, allows for such phenomena as responsible drinking and inappropriate abstinence.[1]

For those who have equated drinking with drunkenness and drunkenness with alcoholism, some ideas of the newer interpretation will seem outrageous, heretical, and at the very least, contradictory. But Americans have lived a long time with basic contradictions pertaining to alcohol use and nonuse. While drinking practices suggest that most Americans are wet (they are drinkers), attitudes indicate that many of these same drinkers have very definite guilt feelings or apprehensions about alcohol use. There is a real unwillingness to admit that what one does in or through drinking is pleasurable or legitimate. Is this an instance of behavioral change preceding attitudinal change?

It should be remembered, then, as the several dimensions of the alcohol story are described, that the chief concern is the human experience with its motivations, attitudes, values and ecologic interactions with the environment. *One element of that environment is alcohol, but alcohol alone does not create problems. People themselves constitute problems.*

---

[1]For a revolutionary approach to the entire range of problems related to alcohol use and recommendations for their solution, the reader should consult the report of The Cooperative Commission on the Study of Alcoholism, *Alcohol Problems: A Report to the Nation*, A study prepared by Thomas F. A. Plant (New York: Oxford University Press, 1967).

Figure 1. For a variety of reasons and with a measure of moderation, a majority of Americans engage in drinking, while a significant minority refrains from alcohol use. (Reprinted with permission of the Licensed Beverage Industries, Inc. Source: Seagram Distillers Co.)

They disagree, sometimes very vehemently, about the use and nonuse of alcohol; they have many difficulties dealing with the results of drinking behavior.

Prevalence of Alcohol Use

The first dimension of the problem deals with the impact of alcohol on American life. Current estimates of the number of drinkers, age fifteen and over, reveal that there are approximately ninety-three million Americans who partake of alcoholic beverages to some extent.[2] Thus, the drinking age population of the United States constitutes nearly 71 per cent of the total adult population.[3]

Additional statistics indicate that the yearly consumption of alcoholic beverages (including beer, wine and distilled spirits) per capita of the

---

[2]Consumption estimates are frequently based on selected samplings of the adult population, or on the amount of tax-paid alcoholic beverages delivered by the manufacturer to a distributor.

[3]Vera Efron and Mark Keller, *Selected Statistical Tables on the Consumption of Alcohol, 1950-1962 and on Alcoholism, 1930-1960,* and yearly supplements thereto (New Brunswick, N. J.: Rutgers Center of Alcohol Studies, 1963).

drinking age population approaches twenty-six U. S. gallons, of which slightly over two gallons are total absolute alcohol. At first glance, such figures seem alarming indeed. But just a single six pack of beer, each week for a year, does add up to a considerable volume. Few people, though, would consider this to be a case of excessive drinking. On the other hand, it is probable that the relatively heavy drinkers and alcoholics purchase far more alcoholic beverages than the moderate drinkers. As one recovered alcoholic once remarked to a drinking friend, "I spilled more in one week than you drank in one year."

The annual price tag for all alcoholic beverages approximates eleven billion dollars or nearly 3 per cent of all personal consumption expenditures. Recently, in one midwestern state the per capita spending for

50% TAXES TO GOVERNMENT.

Figure 2. Doctors agree that moonshine can cripple, blind, and kill. Illegally produced distilled spirits often contain poisonous substances. The containers above are part of a 120 gallon moonshine stash recently seized in Jefferson County, Alabama. (Reprinted with permission of the Alcohol and Tobacco Tax Division, Internal Revenue Service, U. S. Treasury Department.)

Figure 3. $5,000 per day tax fraud. This is part of a mammouth moonshining operation found in a Union County, North Carolina, barn by law enforcement agents. The still was capable of turning out 500 gallons of non-tax-paid liquor every day and had been in operation from one to two weeks. The vats shown here contained 12,000 gallons of filth-ridden mash. (Reprinted with permission of the Licensed Beverage Industries, Inc.)

distilled spirits alone amounted to twenty-seven dollars a year. Although every state and the federal government attempt to control the manufacture and sale of beverage alcohol, the contribution of alcohol revenues to governmental coffers totals about five billion dollars annually—a rather substantial sum.

In general, the mass media sanction and approve the moderate use of alcohol as a part of everyday living. Indeed, some television programs depict drinking not only as an integral part of the good life, but as a social obligation.

At the present time, all fifty states provide for the legal sale and consumption of beverage alcohol. Mississippi, the last state to prohibit the legal sale of distilled spirits, repealed its prohibition law in 1966. Definite restrictions, including local option, persist in most areas. The illegal activities of moonshining (illicit production of distilled spirits) and bootlegging (secret and unlawful transportation and sale of beverage alcohol) also persist.

Alcohol's Impact on Society

Alcohol commands a rather significant place in society. The following evidence is offered:

1. The only amendment to the United States Constitution that has ever been repealed was the Prohibition Amendment (the Eighteenth Amendment which was repealed by the Twenty-first Amendment). *1920*
2. One of the most popular musicians held in esteem by the older generation has Champagne Musicmakers, a Champagne Lady and bubbles by the billions. *1933*
3. Performing artists generate a mystical alcoholic appeal through their tranquilized manner, their proclamation of "how sweet it is" and their lovable imitation of intoxicated persons, much to the delight of audiences.
4. The first rebellion to confront the infant federal government was the Whiskey Rebellion of 1794.
5. Modern drama, novels, television plays and films frequently deal with some aspect of alcohol, particularly alcoholism.
6. Numerous songs that pertain to alcohol and drinking are represented by Broadway showstoppers, college classics and popular tunes. And of course, you can probably recall those "99 bottles of beer on the wall" or a similar ditty.
7. Newly constructed ships are launched with champagne, not soft drinks with one, crazy calorie.
8. When the housewife puts on one of her fancy dresses for the evening, she refers to it as a cocktail dress.

Additionally, one might consider the numerous breweries that sponsor the broadcasts and telecasts of sporting events; the vast acreage of

1. Statistics support the view that per capita alcohol consumption is extremely high. Are these statistics subject to misinterpretation? How do you interpret those given in this chapter?
2. Why is government interest in moonshine high? Why do illegal stills and bootlegging persist?
3. Is drinking a social obligation? Is it essential under certain circumstances? If so, when?
4. How does current advertising promote alcohol consumption?

farmlands devoted to the growing of grain, grapes and hops; and the complex of commercial enterprises concerned with the manufacture, distribution and sale of beverage alcohol. Indeed, alcohol has, is and will continue to play a king-size role in America, a drinking society.

One fact seems of paramount importance. The drinking of alcoholic beverages is an established custom in America. For a variety of reasons and with a measure of moderation, a majority of persons engage in drinking, while a significant minority refrain from alcohol use. *Young persons growing up in such a society, however, are likely to embrace the prevailing adult pattern. In fact, they do.*

CHAPTER 2

Some Alcohol Problems

If alcohol itself is not the major problem, a claim made earlier, why do so many alcohol problems seem to exist? Perhaps this question can be answered partially by citing Jackson's analysis of social problems and alcoholic beverages.[1] She contends that the use of alcohol as a problem arises from (1) the prevailing values of the culture; (2) the inability of the intoxicated person to display socially acceptable behavior; (3). the inadequacy and inefficiency of social controls.

A person's value system will determine whether alcohol is perceived as an intrinsic evil or as one of nature's gifts to be enjoyed. The unacceptable behavior of the drunk is so judged not by the intoxicated person himself, but by those who view him. And teenage drinking presents a difficult situation for many communities because of the unenforceability of current laws. Truly, people not only originate major social problems, but to a large degree perpetuate them.

This second dimension of the alcohol story is concerned with the so-called problems related to beverage alcohol. In the brief discussion which follows, the contrasting and often contradictory nature of American attitudes and practices regarding alcohol use will be described.[2]

The Churches and Alcohol Use

The use of beverage alcohol has been a major issue with some religious denominations for many years. Many Protestant faiths in America have been identified with the Temperance Movement, which evolved into a morality of total abstinence during the midnineteenth century in the United States. Traditionally, the more ascetic groups for-

---

[1]Joan K. Jackson, "Assumptions Regarding Social Disorganization and Alcohol," *Alcohol Education for Classroom and Community*, ed., Raymond G. McCarthy (New York: McGraw-Hill Book Company, 1964), p. 154.

[2]For a detailed analysis of various alcohol problems, the reader is directed to *Alcohol Problems: A Report to the Nation* and *Alcohol Education for Classroom and Community, op. cit.* Basic concepts from each text have been incorporated in the present chapter.

Figure 4. Moderate drinking: integrated with routines related to leisure activities, eating, and social functions. (Reprinted with permission of the Licensed Beverage Industries, Inc. Source: Seagram Distillers Co.)

bade drinking as sinful and equated occasional drinking with inebriation, the former being the initial stage of the latter. This statement should not be construed as an adequate description of all or even most Protestant bodies, some of which have always approved the use of alcoholic beverages in moderation. While all churches deplore drunkeness, there is no consensus on what constitutes moderation. Furthermore, some denominations have recently reversed their total-abstinence stand and now concentrate on the necessity of avoiding dangerous forms of drinking. Abstinence, though, is often represented as the ideal conduct and is frequently urged for church members.

In opposition to what some might term the *antialcohol bias* of the abstinent or "dry" church groups are the Jews and Catholics. Both faiths condemn drunkenness, but both groups employ the use of alcohol in religious ceremonies. In some Jewish homes, the use of wine is symbolic of family unity and God's goodness to mankind. For both, the temperate or moderate use of alcohol is approved, although total abstinence is not discouraged. Additionally, many members of both groups regard the moderate use of alcoholic beverages as acceptable ways of promoting sociability. Here too the precise definition of moderate drinking is subject to individual interpretation.

Views on Intoxication

Such basic disagreement about alcohol usage is also apparent in the unpredictable reaction of persons to the inebriate. Some express horror and contempt; others laugh or joke about the situation. On occasion, these opposite reactions can be forthcoming in the same situation. An example would be the intoxicated roommate who returns to his residence hall early Saturday morning. The results of his beer blast are more than tolerated until he begins to experience reverse peristalsis, or vomits. Equally peculiar is the failure of most persons to assume any responsibility for the conduct of the drunken person. Little thought is ever given to such a minimal action as refusing to serve another drink to an intoxicated person who is attending a party, apparently because this would diminish the social atmosphere. One wonders how many still subscribe to the dictum of being your brother's keeper.

The Guilty Drinker

Another difficulty that is evident is the guilt complex mentioned in the first chapter. More than one drinker has expressed qualms about purchasing alcoholic beverages in a state store or other public place. Even though he is making a legal purchase of a legal product, he feels uncomfortable or even embarrassed if someone else recognizes him. Why should this be? Has the antialcohol education of church or school had some real carry-over value? Or has the nation not fully recovered from the prohibition era in which the manufacture, distribution and sale of alcoholic beverages were illegal? The idea that drinking is wrong still persists, even for some drinkers.

A variant form of the guilt feeling or apprehension about alcohol use stems from the person who has grown up in an environment of strict abstinence. Later, he becomes involved in a social situation in which under pressure, he feels he must drink. By doing so, he is placed in direct opposition to his family and his value system.

Still another form of guilt, or paradoxical situation, is generated by some parents who caution their own children about the harmful and evil effects of alcohol while they themselves partake of their before dinner drinks. It is an instance of talking out of one side of the mouth and sipping out of the other. This is comparable to the smoking parent who condemns his child for smoking. Is this parental hypocrisy, or misdirection of youth?

Public Aspects of Alcohol Use

When such basic disagreement and conflict exist in matters of the morality of alcohol use, the definition of moderation and personal reactions to drunkenness, plus the guilt feelings, there is bound to be no accord or harmony in dealing with the public aspects of alcohol usage.

The following phenomena are representative of such ambivalence:

1. *Conflicting state laws which regulate the sale of beverage alcohol.* Most states have established the minimum age levels for the purchase of alcoholic beverages at twenty-one years, yet New York and Louisiana have lowered the age limit to eighteen. In nearly half the states, there are no provisions under which minors may consume beverage alcohol legally, but some permit its legal use with parental consent, in the presence of a parent, or if prescribed by a physician. While some states permit alcoholic beverages to be sold by licensed groceries and drug stores, other states restrict the sale to state-operated stores. A few states even prohibit the sale of alcohol by-the-drink in public places. And in others, if the Sunday prohibition on the sale of distilled spirits begins to hurt convention business, hotel bars are permitted to post "open" signs. While most reasonable persons recognize the necessity of laws regulating the use of alcohol, the current crazy-quilt pattern of controls generates a good deal of confusion, especially among youth.

2. *Confusion over methods of handling those persons who become intoxicated in public.* If these persons are chronic alcoholics—and many of them are—are they responsible for their behavior? If they are sick, suffering from the illness of alcoholism, can they in justice be jailed for a criminal offense? If they ought not be jailed, what should be done with them? Court rulings in the United States District Courts of Appeals in Richmond and in the District of Columbia during 1966 stipulated that detention for treatment and rehabilitation is preferred, but no criminal conviction may follow. However, in 1968, the United States Supreme Court refused to prohibit the jailing of alcoholics in a 5-to-4 vote, landmark decision which reaffirmed the attitude that public drunkenness is a criminal act.

3. *Basic disagreement* and, in some places, sharp conflict *over the nature of alcohol education* in the public schools.[3] What is it that young persons are expected to know, feel and do about alcohol? If the focus is on abstinence, the school is placed in sharp conflict with the folkways of the majority. If the chief concern is with moderation, the school might be accused of fostering teenage drinking in opposition to state laws. If the focus is on alcoholism only, the adequacy of education for potential drinkers who will not become problem drinkers, about 95 per cent of the drinking population, is questionable.

4. *Inability to set priorities in an attempt to decrease alcohol problems.* What is the most serious alcohol problem? Adults frequently cite the terrible consequences of teenage drinking. Law enforcement authorities express concern for public drunkenness and driving while intoxicated. Professional health personnel too frequently identify alcoholism as the

---

[3]The reader is referred to a modern and realistic approach to this problem by Hilma Unterberger and Lena Di Cicco, "Alcohol Education Re-evaluated," *The Bulletin of the National Association of Secondary School Principals*, 52:15-29, 1968.

number one issue. This lack of consensus takes its toll in a confused public. There is the disinclination of persons to become involved in emotional dialogue and the underfunding of public and voluntary health agencies dealing with alcohol problems. Such conditions persist because the causes and nature of problem drinking, including alcoholism, are not entirely understood, even from a scientific point of view. Alcoholism alone has been labeled as (1) an expression of immorality; (2) a basic personality defect; (3) a disease process; (4) a personal health problem; (5) a sociolegal problem.

(5) *Persistence in the belief that the major reason for all drinking among young persons is the expression of hostility toward or defiance of adult authority.* All the significant research on attitudes and practices of teenagers regarding alcohol use indicates that adolescents drink primarily in imitation of the adult drinking pattern. Closely related to this aspect is the belief that all teenage drinkers are problem drinkers. Again, research suggests that problem drinking is actually quite low among adolescents. While most have tasted or experimented with beverage alcohol, the typical young drinker rarely drinks on a daily basis and is most likely to have been introduced to drinking in his own home and with parental consent, if not encouragement. But why do many adults tend to stereotype all teenage drinking as irresponsible and excessive?

(6) *The continuing belief that the use of alcohol is the direct cause of impoverishment, desertion, racial strife, divorce, neglect, dependence on welfare agencies, juvenile delinquency, civil disobedience, and illegal and antisocial behavior of adults.* Even when the use of alcohol has been disproven, this national scapegoat is still suspect as the number one cause of major social problems. A more scientific and realistic relationship between alcohol and social issues is described as multifactorial and circular. For instance, inharmonious interpersonal relationships or some personality imbalance interacts with drinking, thus giving rise to further disruption of family relationships and personality integration, and to further problem drinking. Nevertheless, the simple cause of our problems is identified as "king alcohol" and the simple solution can be found in its prohibition. This all too frequent reaction is a prime example of the American tendency to overuse the common mental mechanism of projection.

The author's intent in setting forth the conflicts and peculiarities, as noted above, is not to level criticism at Americans because of their individual interpretations or their real concern for personal rights. Rather, the purpose is one of acknowledging some basic inconsistencies and the contrasting sentiments that exist in the nation today. However, once acknowledged, these differences might be seen as major obstacles in effectively combatting problem drinking, in developing effective programs of education to prevent the results of excessive drinking and in devising appropriate and·enforceable laws which regulate the use of alcoholic beverages. Could it be that our diversities thwart the development of an environment less conducive to abnormal drinking?

CHAPTER 3

Use and Nonuse
of Beverage Alcohol

"I can't really see what all the fuss is about. You either drink or you don't."

This common response of a student to a teacher's inquiry about personal decision-making and alcohol use is quite revealing. It leads one to wonder if any conscious decision to initiate drinking is ever made. The same remark, further developed, usually indicates that young persons look upon a decision to drink as a permanent one. Furthermore, the response suggests that scant attention is given to additional decisions concerning use and nonuse of alcohol.

Decision-making in a Drinking Culture

In reality, living in a drinking culture demands repeated decision-making on the part of both those who use and those who refrain from using alcoholic beverages. For instance, a responsible drinker might consider how to ingest beverage alcohol so as to avoid intoxication. It is hoped that such a drinker would act favorably upon the realization that there are certain circumstances in which the use of any alcoholic beverage is unsuitable or potentially hazardous. Additionally, there are decisions to be made about how much one will drink and with whom one will drink. The user might also take a variety of actions to protect his right or privilege to drink. Inevitably, the drinking parent is confronted with the question of fostering, disapproving, or tolerating the use of alcoholic beverages among his children. And what about the decisions of the host at a party where drinking is a major activity? Provisions might be made for those guests who do not use alcohol and for those known alcoholics who might be in attendance. Perhaps the host would restrict the continued consumption on the part of an intoxicated guest and arrange for his safe transportation home. And then, of course, a drinker could always decide to revert to abstinence.

On the other hand, the nondrinker must frequently make repeated decisions pertaining to alcohol, because he normally interacts with those who do use beverage alcohol, either as neighbors, drinking drivers, business associates or in some other capacity. Nonuse probably determines the abstainer's behavior toward people who drink. If a person feels strongly about his nonuse, he might not attend a social function which attracts mostly drinkers. Abstaining hosts decide whether or not to procure and serve alcoholic drinks to their drinking guests. The nonuser, like his drinking counterpart, also influences the attitudes and practices of his children. Through his decision at the ballot box, the nondrinker frequently decides whether his friends and neighbors will be able to purchase alcoholic beverages in a particular geographical location. One can only speculate as to how many nondrinking jury members are influenced by the knowledge of a defendant's drinking practices. And finally, the nondrinker consents, either passively or in frustrated opposition, to help foot the "bill of abuse" in increased auto-insurance premiums and rehabilitation services for alcoholics. *Indeed, there are many decisions that can be made, including the one to drink.*

But what prompts people to drink in the first place? And just as important, why do so many millions prefer to remain nondrinkers? The answers might be found in an analysis of the phenomenon called drinking.

The Nature of Drinking

By definition, drinking is the ingestion or consumption of beverages which contain ethyl alcohol. In a drinking society, however, young persons typically grow up as nondrinkers. Although most of these nondrinking children are exposed to drinking parents and relatives, and other influences of a drinking culture, the option of incorporating drinking into one's life pattern probably does not occur until age thirteen or fourteen. It is at this time, as Russell suggests, that decisions about continued use or nonuse determine new forms of interaction with alcohol, which in turn will affect the future growth and development style of the individual.[1] If physiological and psychological reactions to alcohol use are interpreted as pleasing or advantageous, the experimenter will become a user. Such a concept-centered, circular interpretation of drinking practices also allows for the experimenter who returns to nonuse, and the person who maintains his abstinence status all along.

In a sociological interpretation, Bacon describes drinking as a particular group's customary ways of ingesting beverage alcohol.[2] Such a custom is learned by other members of that group and is perpetuated by the group because drinking serves to promote sociality. The pleasure derived from drinking is primarily reciprocal, for example, drinking by

[1]Robert D. Russell, "A New Way of Thinking About Alcohol," *Journal of Alcohol Education*, 12:25-28, 1966.
[2]Selden D. Bacon, "Alcoholics Do Not Drink," *The Annals of the American Academy of Political and Social Science*, 315:55-64, 1958.

one of the group brings satisfaction to the other drinkers. For Americans, this social drinking is the common way of imbibing alcoholic beverages.

Common Reasons for Use of Beverage Alcohol

The particular forms of pleasure derived from drinking are many and varied:

1. Drinking is a tradition which identifies one with a particular group or culture. A sense of belonging is fostered when family groups celebrate important events, some joyful and some sad, with some form of drinking activity. It must be mentioned that some persons consider a meal to be incomplete unless some type of beverage alcohol is served. For them, beer and wine are integral parts of a normal diet. Additionally, drinking might be seen as an act of conformity which results in group acceptance, as occurs in some youth circles.

2. Drinking can produce a tranquilizing effect which reduces tension and anxiety. Stressful situations are more easily tolerated; irritations of everyday living seem to diminish; relaxation is facilitated. Quite a few persons look upon alcohol as the preferred way of dealing with increased pressures of modern living. Perhaps, then, the foremost reason for drinking is to alter one's feeling. It should be noted that some members of the younger generation claim that alcohol is the older generation's form of marijuana.

3. Many persons claim that they drink because they like the taste of alcoholic beverages. That thirst-quenching taste of golden brew on a hot day is unbeatable, although one wonders how many would purchase a simulated alcoholic beverage with the alcohol removed. Could it be that the effect of the drink is at least as important as the taste?

4. Alcohol has been described as the "social lubricant" in which the superego is dissolved. For some, then, drinking is a means of lowering or releasing the inhibitions of caution, reserve and suspicion which characterize many human relationships.

5. Because the use of beverage alcohol is so prevalent in America, drinking becomes symbolic of adult status. Young persons in particular claim that drinking makes them feel important and grown-up. Unfortunately, the use of a symbol of maturity is too often equated with being mature.

6. Another motive for drinking is related to the "forbidden fruit" aspect which appeals to adolescents. Great delight is apparent when a law can be broken and no penalty is forthcoming. There is something which approaches mild excitement in "beating the law."

7. Drinking is also a symbol of prosperity, affluence and personal success. Perceived as such, beverage alcohol is often used to create an atmosphere of sophistication at parties or important dinners. The connoisseur of fine wines and distilled spirits most often enjoys a considerable reputation or prestige.

It should be noted that the several forms of pleasure derived from the use of alcohol, as cited above, are most frequently achieved through social drinking. This does not mean that solitary drinking per se is abnormal or pathological. As a matter of fact, many instances of social drinking have disastrous consequences. But the reasons given for solitary drinking often suggest that it is engaged in for its own sake. Reliance on alcohol to escape from the realm of reality via intoxication or to escape boredom does not fit easily into the picture of customary social drinking. Similarly, drinking which is symbolic of rebellion against parental authority or religious discipline is not common to social drinking, except with some adolescents. But in such an instance, other motivations are probably operable in the social setting. Increasing dependence on chemical crutches to meet the problems of daily living is viewed with alarm by many authorities.

Common Reasons for Nonuse of Beverage Alcohol

Just as there are numerous reasons for drinking, the motivations for nonuse of alcoholic beverages are equally worthy and extensive, and also suggest that a certain pleasure is associated with abstinence. Reasons for nonuse of alcohol are as follows:

1. The nonuse of alcohol is a tradition with many individuals. Just as drinking serves to identify with a particular group, abstinence has a similar function.

2. Nonuse may represent a religious belief that drinking is wrong or detrimental. However, spiritual motives for nonuse may include the aspect of self-denial and the desire not to harm others by one's drinking example. Hoff describes these latter motives for abstaining as sincere and noble ways of loving and serving God.[3]

3. Some persons prefer not to drink because they wish to face reality without a psychological crutch. A spirit of adventure or independence is generated and a certain pride is established in being able to tackle the problems of living without the tranquilizing effect of alcohol.

4. Abstinence for some represents a desire to retain human performance at peak level. One way to assure the efficiency of motor skills and the keeness of judgment is to avoid the depressant effect of beverage alcohol. This is a significant factor when one enumerates the hazards of a modern, complex society. Often, man at his best is not good enough, as in driving an automobile or in performing certain critical occupational skills. The effects of alcohol on human performance do not seem to improve the situation.

---

[3]Ebbe Curtis Hoff, *Decisions About Alcohol* (New York: The Seabury Press, 1961), pp. 42-45.

5. Some persons do not use alcohol in order to avoid the risks of drunkenness and alcoholism. In addition to sustaining a motor vehicle accident, the immediate consequences of intoxication can include the alienation of friends, a ruined reputation, loss of a business contract, an unwanted sexual experience, the hangover, public arrest and personal injury. As far as alcoholism is concerned, the odds are known: One in fifteen who drink will become an alcoholic.

6. The nonuse of beverage alcohol can often be related to factors of health, such as diabetes and alcoholism, or to a general dislike of the taste and the irritating and depressant effects on the individual.

7. Last, but not least, is the economics of drinking which may be sufficient to promote abstinence. Just one dollar per week spent on alcoholic beverages seems to be an insignificant sum. But over a ten-year period, the cost multiplies to $500; in a fifty-year lifetime of such moderate drinking, the bill comes to $2,500, a healthy savings, inflation notwithstanding.

Undoubtedly, the pros and cons listed above do not tell the whole story. Perhaps the reader can identify other pleasures or motivations associated with use, nonuse or even abuse of beverage alcohol. The questions, though, must be posed: How often is one's drinking or abstaining the result of intelligent decision-making? Does one really know why he uses or refrains from using alcohol? Does one really care?

Some Pertinent Issues

No analysis of the reasons for and against drinking would be adequate without a brief commentary on some important issues of a drinking culture, characterized by *Time Magazine* as more "moist" than either "wet" or "dry."[4]

Education about abstinence today is impaired by at least two factors: 1. the heavy overtones of morality frequently associated with nonuse; 2. the overpowering proalcohol influences of a drinking culture. Indeed, it has become difficult to convince young persons that nonuse of alcoholic beverages is still a viable alternative to drinking. *The big "hang-up" seems to be in helping persons learn to say no, without embarrassment, when offered an alcoholic beverage.* Some reasonable and lighthearted excuses for abstaining might include: "Sorry, but I prefer a Bloody Shame"; (an alcohol-free Bloody Mary) or "Not now, I'm in training for basketball season"; or "No thanks, I can get the same effect by removing my contact lenses."

Another issue concerns *the matter of civil rights and the use or nonuse of alcohol.* Many persons among the nearly thirty-eight million abstainers in America resent the pressure and expectation to drink at

---

[4]"Time Essay: How America Drinks," *Time,* December 29, 1967, p. 15.

social functions. It seems as if the nondrinkers are discriminated against by their abstention. Of course, during the period of national prohibition (1920-1933) the situation was reversed to a degree. What a difference fifty years make! Nevertheless, refusal to drink often generates suspicion, mistrust, even ridicule. Ideally, pressure to drink should be absent, and the nonuse of alcoholic beverages should be more than tolerated. It should be respected.

There is another side of the coin. The nonuser of beverage alcohol easily assumes the role of a self-righteous teetotaler. He frequently wishes to impose his abstinence on those who drink. Those who use alcohol are the "devil incarnate," and most deserving of hellfire if they persist in such an evil habit. Such behavior may have been in vogue at one time, but today's divergent and uncompromising issues seem more within the sphere of reason if men of goodwill agree to disagree agreeably.

Recently, another form of discrimination has been recognized with regard to alcohol use. For a society that in many ways encourages drinking, those who cannot control such activity are the victims of disinterest, apathy, "persecution," too little care and not enough treatment or rehabilitation. *The real outcasts of the drinking culture are the problem drinkers*. How responsive have we been to the genuine needs of these persons? What responsibility does the drinking society, both users and nonusers, owe to those who abuse alcohol?

Alcohol has often been cast as the "bloody villain" that defiles innocence. There is no doubt that some young persons engage in sexual intercourse for the first time while they are under the influence of beverage alcohol. Such activity is only one example of the bizarre and irresponsible behavior frequently displayed by those who drink immoderately. The matter of civil rights arises again in relation to the exploitative use of alcohol. How many times has a person been "liquored-up" so that he or she may be more easily seduced? Alcohol can be employed to exploit persons in nonsexual matters too. Consider the youth who asks his father for money or the use of the family car only after good, old dad has belted down two or three drinks; and the businessman who knows that "bottled happiness" and a "gay" client will more likely result in a signed contract. Can the reader think of any other ways in which alcohol is used to exploit other individuals?

Some Pertinent Definitions

From the evidence presented thus far, the continuum of drinking practices can be seen as including nonuse, use and abuse of alcoholic beverages. Three special terms pertinent to such a continuum can now be explained in the light of a value orientation.

1. *Irresponsible nonuse.* This term, attributed to Unterberger and Di Cicco, refers mostly to the motivations people have for abstaining.[5] Unreasonable fears of the consequences of drinking are considered "unhealthy." To anticipate an overpowering addiction following one sip of beverage alcohol is a denial of scientific findings to the contrary. Likewise, the coach's ban on drinking because of its permanent effects on player efficiency can no longer be based on evidence which does not exist. Athletes would probably respond more to abstinence based on group self-denial. And then, of course, there is the notorious abstainer who insists upon having more "fun" at a party and "flying high," without alcohol, than the drinkers.

2. *Moderate drinking.* Frequently used to describe nondisruptive and controlled use of alcoholic beverages, moderate drinking, like irresponsible nonuse, is most difficult to define. Moderate drinking is usually descriptive of social drinking, but the limits of propriety are likely to vary from one group to another. However, most "alcohologists" agree that acceptable drinking is governed by the nature and extent of the drinker's responsibilities. Since everyone has some responsibilities in this complex age—either to himself, his family or to other members of society—moderate drinking implies limitation of alcohol use. Todd identifies three dimensions of this limitation, namely, quantity, time and effect.[6] "Quantity" may range from one drink to several; "time" may include both daily drinking and drinking confined to infrequent occasions; "effect" encompasses not only physical health, but areas of psychological and social health, and economics. *If one can drink within the elastic range of such limitation, avoid intoxication, and not cause significant damage to himself, his family and the total community because of such drinking, he is probably engaging in moderate drinking.*

With the expectation of criticism and the admission of incompleteness, the following additional characteristics of moderate drinking are offered:

1. Drinking is integrated with routines related to leisure activities, eating and social functions.
2. Drinking is motivated by reasons which not only produce temporary adjustment, but facilitate future solutions of problems and personality integration.
3. Drinking is conducted among friends or within the family setting.
4. Drinking is "paced" by ingesting beverages slowly. (Try sipping.) The second drink is consumed no sooner than one hour after the first; the third no sooner than one hour after the second.
5. Drinking on an empty stomach is avoided by ingesting cream, milk, ice cream, meat, eggs or cheese before ingesting alcoholic beverages.

---

[5]Unterberger and Di Cicco, *op. cit.*, pp. 17-18.
[6]Frances Todd, *Teaching About Alcohol* (New York: McGraw-Hill Book Company, 1964), p. 95.

1. Few youngsters like the taste of beer the first time they try it. Why do they try it again?
2. It's true that drinking and driving don't mix, yet a host hardly expects all his guests to stay overnight. How might the drinking guests avert the danger of driving?
3. Many students can't afford to take a taxi home every time they attend drinking parties. What alternatives would you suggest for them?

3. *Problem drinking.*[7] This term like the other two above, is subject to many and varied interpretations. Depending on who is doing the defining, the following persons might be problem drinkers: anyone who drinks, the abstainer, the "light drinker," "the heavy drinker," the drinker of distilled spirits and the teenager who drinks. For many the definition appears to be the major problem. But more realistically, ". . . the problem drinkers are those who—by all standards—cause significant damage to themselves, their families, or their communities because of drinking."[8]

The problem drinker, unlike the majority of users, will not or cannot consume alcoholic beverages without generating some difficulty for himself or others. Such abusers are estimated to constitute about 10 per cent of all drinkers in the United States.[9]

Some hallmarks of problem drinking are listed below:

1. Drinking in excess of customary dietary or social use.
2. Drinking which is motivated by a need to feel important or to cure a feeling of depression.
3. Drinking which is engaged in for its own sake or because of a desire to escape from reality or boredom or because one cannot get through the day without a drink.
4. Drinking which is adjustive, for example, tension-reducing but not conducive to long-term problem-solving. An example of this phenomenon would be the person who persistently solves the problem of a nagging wife via alcohol. Temporary relief is achieved by drinking; the wife seems more tolerable, but the long-term quality of the marital relationship is probably endangered. The nagging wife remains, and the reasons the wife nags remain!
5. Drinking *without* regard to the responsibilities of the drinker or to the demands of his occupation, including the operation of a motor vehicle, piloting a jumbo jet, performing a heart transplant, programming a computer, or supervising children.

---

[7]The area of problem drinking, including alcoholism, will be treated in greater depth in Chapter 6.

[8]National Center for Prevention and Control of Alcoholism, National Institute of Mental Health, *Alcohol and Alcoholism* (U. S. Government Printing Office, 1967), p. 5.

[9]*Ibid.*, p. 10.

CHAPTER 4

Alcoholic Beverages

Alcohol is the term which describes a chemical compound, ethyl alcohol. It is the essential and characteristic ingredient of beverage alcohol. Ethyl alcohol or ethanol distinguishes this beverage from all others. While there are various uses for ethyl alcohol in industry and medicine, concern here is with alcohol and drinking.

The Nature of Ethyl Alcohol

Ethyl alcohol is only one of many chemical substances classified as alcohols. Others include methyl alcohol, n-propyl alcohol and n-butyl alcohol. Each has a different chemical makeup and each has different properties, but all alcohols are intoxicating if consumed in certain amounts. Methyl alcohol, or wood alcohol is particularly toxic, because the body cannot easily dispose of the substance. In addition, the combustion product of methyl alcohol, unlike ethyl alcohol, can damage the body's nerves. Frequently, the optic nerve is injured and blindness results. The chemical composition and physical properties of ethyl alcohol make it relatively more safe for human consumption than the other alcohols.

The chemical formula for ethyl alcohol is C_2H_5OH, indicating that a molecule of the compound is composed of two carbon atoms, five hydrogen atoms and one hydroxyl OH group. From a chemical point of view, ethyl alcohol is similar to ether and shares with that substance an anesthetic effect on the central nervous system.

Some of the common properties of ethyl alcohol are: a thin, clear, colorless fluid; mild, aromatic odor; miscible with water in all proportions; insoluble in dry proteins and minerals; diffusible through body membranes; and, pungent taste. Initially, ethyl alcohol has a burning or irritating effect on the lining of the oral cavity and esophagus. Its primary pharmacological effect is depression of the central nervous system.

Figure 5. Hallmark of problem drinking: ingestion of alcohol in excess of customary dietary or social use. In spite of unique qualities, drinking has its limitations and possible dangers. (Reprinted with permission of the State of Florida Alcoholic Rehabilitation Program)

Fermentation

The ethyl alcohol contained in alcoholic beverages is derived from certain grains and fruits by fermentation. One of nature's chemical reactions, *fermentation,* is a process in which yeast cells act on the sugar content of fruit juice and convert the sugar to carbon dioxide and alcohol. The following simplified equation represents the fermentation process:

$$\underset{\text{glucose (sugar)}}{C_6H_{12}O_6} \xrightarrow{\text{Yeast}} \underset{\text{ethyl alcohol}}{2C_2H_5OH} \quad + \quad \underset{\text{carbon dioxide}}{2CO_2}$$

Fermentation continues until all the sugar has been acted on by the yeast cells or until the fermenting mixture contains approximately 14 per cent alcohol by volume. At this point, the concentration of ethyl alcohol is sufficient to cause the yeast cells to stop functioning.

Figure 6. These open fermenters contain beer in an early state of fermentation. The production of carbon dioxide induced by action of the yeast already is taking place. (Reprinted with permission of the United States Brewers Association, Inc.)

Classifications of Alcoholic Beverages

No one normally consumes pure alcohol. Ingestion of ethyl alcohol is accomplished in the form of beverages. These alcoholic beverages have assumed unusual, popular names, such as, *whing dinger, scoops, schooners, cactus juice, curse-your-mommy, hooch, booze, moonshine, white lightning, white mule, bootleg, jolt, mountain dew* and *firewater,* to name a few. While such terms might "enrich" the vocabulary, they are not precise. Alcoholic beverages are generally classified as either wines, beers or distilled spirits.

Wine is most often made from the juice of grapes, but other fruits or berries can be used. The yeast, present in the air and on the skin of the grapes, converts the natural sugar of the juice into alcohol and carbon dioxide. Fermentation proceeds for several days at a warm temperature until the alcohol content of the mixture is between 10 to 14 per cent. If all the natural sugar has been fermented, the resulting wine is referred

Figure 7. Giant fermenting tanks pictured here are used to prepare the whisky mash for the distillation process. (Reprinted with permission of the Licensed Beverage Industries, Inc. Source: Brown-Forman Distillers Corp.)

to as "dry." If the fermentation process is stopped before going to completion, some sugar remains in the mixture, which is described as "sweet" wine.

Not content with ordinary table wines that soon turned to vinegar, people of earlier centuries added plain alcohol or brandy to wines before the fermentation process stopped. This not only prevented the formation of vinegar, but increased the alcohol content of the wines. Such "fortified" wines have an alcohol content as high as 24 per cent. Sherries, vermouths and aperitifs are examples of "fortified" or cocktail wines familiar to American wine drinkers.[1]

In the production of most wines, the carbon dioxide gas escapes. However, when partially fermented grape juice is bottled before the fermentation process is completed, a champagne or sparkling wine is the result. The dissolved carbon dioxide is seen as bubbles when the bottle is opened. Champagne has an alcohol content of approximately 12 per cent. Because carbon dioxide tends to relax the pylorus, the opening

[1]Connoisseurs of wine will be fascinated by the evaluative article, "Cocktail Wines," *Consumer Reports*, June, 1968, pp. 313-319.

between the stomach and small intestine, sparkling wines pass readily from the stomach to the intestine, where rapid absorption occurs.

In contrast to wines, *beers* are derived from cereals, namely, barley, rye, corn and wheat. The process of beer-making is referred to as brewing, and the resultant product contains from 3 to 6 per cent alcohol by volume. Three stages of brewing are usually identified: mashing, fermentation and storage.

Mashing is a process whereby the starch of cereal broth is changed to sugar (maltose). Dried hops which impart a bitter taste to beer are added to the mixture, which is then fermented by the addition of brewer's yeast. Fermentation continues for one or two weeks. During storage, solid materials settle out. The clarified fluid is then carbonated and bottled or canned. Substances other than water and alcohol in the beer are called congeners. Dextrins, maltose, certain soluble minerals and vitamins, organic acids, salts and carbon dioxide are common congeners. These congeners, present to some extent in wines also, add some nutritional value.

Ale is also a malted beverage like beer, but the alcohol content is slightly higher. "Near-beer," produced like regular beer, has all alcohol extracted except for 0.06 per cent. Some authorities do not consider "Near-beer" an alcoholic beverage.

The *distilled spirits,* including whisky, vodka, gin and brandy, are made from fermented mixtures which are heated in a still. Because alcohol has a lower boiling point than that of other substances in the fermented mixture, the ethyl alcohol boils off first and its vapors are then cooled and condensed. The distilled fluid has a very high alcohol content along with some water and flavoring ingredients. The alcohol content of distilled spirits is indicated by the term *proof.* The number preceding the word, *proof,* is twice the percentage of alcohol by volume. Thus, a whisky which is labeled as 90-proof, contains 45 per cent alcohol by volume. Most distilled beverages contain between 40 to 50 per cent alcohol by volume.

Whisky is made from cereal grains, such as corn, rye and barley. After the "raw" whiskey is derived from distillation, it is diluted with water and then aged in charred barrels, which imparts a unique flavor. Vodka (pure unflavored alcohol and water) is derived from rye, barley and sometimes potatoes. Gin, a combination of pure ethyl alcohol and water, is often flavored with the oil of juniper berries or orange peel. Brandy is the distillate of fruit wines, namely grape, cherry, peach and blackberry.

While many persons consume distilled spirits, "straight," for example, uncombined with other beverages, or "on-the-rocks," for example, with ice only, others prefer highballs and mixed drinks. Served in a tall glass with ice, a highball is a dilution of whisky or other liquor with water or carbonated beverage. A mixed drink or cocktail, on the other hand, is an admixture of some distilled spirit with different combinations of wine, water, nonalcoholic carbonated beverage, fruit juices or other flavoring.

Servings of Alcoholic Beverages

Each type of alcoholic beverage differs as to alcohol content. Beers occupy the lower end of the spectrum; wines have an intermediate status; the distilled spirits are at the upper extreme. Nevertheless, a typical serving of any one beverage contains approximately the same amount of alcohol, though in varying concentrations. An analysis of the content of alcohol in specific beverages is illustrated in Table 1.

TABLE 1

Quantity of Serving, Per Cent Alcohol by Volume, and Quantity of Alcohol Per Serving of Various Alcoholic Beverages

Beverage	Quantity of Serving	Per Cent Alcohol by Volume	Quantity of Alcohol per Serving
Beer	12.0 oz.	4	0.48 oz.
Beer	12.0 oz.	6	0.72 oz.
Table Wine	5.0 oz.	12	0.60 oz.
Sherry	3.0 oz.	20	0.60 oz.
Highball	1.5 oz.	40	0.60 oz.
Highball	1.5 oz.	50	0.75 oz.
Cocktail	1.5 oz.	40	0.60 oz.
Cocktail	1.5 oz.	50	0.75 oz.

The amount of ethyl alcohol per serving ranges from just under one-half ounce to three-fourths of an ounce. In most cases, it approximates 0.60 ounce, but this small quantity is present in various dilutions. In a serving of beer, for instance, the beverage is a mixture of 20 parts of nonalcoholic fluid to 1 part of ethyl alcohol. The alcoholic "strength" of sherry wine can be expressed as a ratio of nearly 5 parts of nonalcoholic to 1 part of alcoholic fluid. The highball, with its mixture of 5 parts water or carbonated beverage to 1 part whisky, stands in marked contrast with the cocktail and its greater concentration of alcohol. Most frequently served without ice, the manhattan and martini cocktails are two-ounce psychobiological grenades containing about 3 parts of distilled spirits and 1 part vermouth, another alcoholic beverage. Over 40 per cent of each cocktail is likely to be ethyl alcohol.

These sobering facts should be well-known to those who wish to be moderate drinkers, and will assume added significance in the following chapter.

CHAPTER 5

Alcohol Within the Body

Many drinkers view alcoholic beverages in a social context only, for example, alcohol does something for the drinker. In fact, the drinker does something to the alcohol, and the alcohol, in turn, does something to the drinker. This chapter, then, is concerned with these reciprocal actions of man and alcohol within the human body.

There are various ways by which alcohol enters the body. The most normal, of course, is to swallow beverage alcohol. Nevertheless, alcohol can be absorbed from nearly all surfaces of the body, so that inhalation, injection and enema become possible methods of entry.

After swallowing, the beverage is conveyed to the stomach where the process of absorption begins. In absorption, the alcohol passes through the walls of the gastrointestinal tract into the bloodstream. Once in the blood, the alcohol, now greatly diluted, is circulated to all cells of the body, including the brain. Upon absorption and circulation, alcohol undergoes the process of oxidation in which it is destroyed or broken down into nonalcoholic components. The by-products of alcohol oxidation are then eliminated from the body as water and carbon dioxide, together with a small fraction of the alcohol which is eliminated unchanged through the lungs or in perspiration and urine.

Absorption

Unlike other foods, alcohol requires no digestion. It diffuses readily through the walls of the alimentary tract where tiny blood vessels pick up the alcohol. About one-fifth the total alcohol consumed is thus absorbed in the stomach. The major site of absorption, however, is the small intestine. Tabershaw describes the stomach and intestines as major holding areas for alcohol.[1] He further notes that alcohol does not stay

---

[1] Irving R. Tabershaw, "Metabolism of Alcohol," reprinted in *Alcohol and College Youth*, Proceedings of a Conference, Lake Tahoe, California, June 10-12, 1965, (Sponsored by the American College Health Association under a grant from the National Institute of Mental Health), p. 143.

in the gastrointestinal tract for long, because the diffusion rate of alcohol is proportional to alcohol concentration, and there is no limit to the rate of absorption. This is especially true if the stomach is empty.

A number of factors can influence significantly the absorption of alcohol.

Concentration of alcohol.   The greater the concentration of alcohol in a beverage, the more rapid will be the rate of absorption. As a consequence, the concentration of alcohol in the blood will be higher. Given the same quantity of alcoholic beverages, two ounces of whisky will produce a higher blood-alcohol level than two ounces of beer.

Amount of alcohol.   The quantity of beverage consumed is a determining factor in the time required for total absorption. The more alcohol ingested at any one time, the longer the absorption period will be.

Rate of drinking.   The rapid ingestion of beverage alcohol through gulping drinks will likely result in elevated blood-alcohol levels. Drinking in small, divided amounts prevents high concentrations of alcohol. Less alcohol will be available for absorption.

Amount of food in the stomach.   The presence of food in the stomach delays the absorption of alcohol. Ingested alcohol is diluted by the food contents of the stomach which remain for processes of digestion. Thus, alcohol is retained for a longer period in the stomach where absorption occurs more slowly than in the small intestine.

Nonalcoholic substances in alcoholic beverages.   Generally speaking, the more nonalcoholic substances in a beverage, the more slowly will be the absorption of alcohol. These nonalcoholic substances present in beer include water, sugars, salts, soluble minerals and amino acids. They tend to dilute the alcohol and reduce its concentration with results as noted above. Because wine is usually consumed along with meals, absorption is similarly slowed. However, the carbon dioxide present in champagne and sparkling wines actually speeds up absorption. The CO_2 relaxes the pyloric valve, permitting the rapid passage of alcohol from the stomach to the small intestine.

Body weight.   The more a person weighs, the lower will be the blood-alcohol level (the percentage of alcohol in the blood) which results upon the consumption of beverage alcohol. Heavier persons have more body fluids in which the alcohol is diluted. As a consequence, one serving of such a beverage will cause a lower concentration in a large adult than in a smaller person whose dilution factor would be considerably less.

Pylorospasm.   At the juncture of the stomach and the small intestine, there is a muscular valve called the pylorus, or pyloric valve. In some drinkers, the irritation of the pylorus, which controls the passage of food from stomach to intestine, causes the valve to close tightly. This sudden, involuntary muscular contraction is referred to as a spasm and can be caused by the consumption of too much alcohol. Highly concentrated alcohol actually retards absorption in some instances. Consequently, the alcohol remains in the stomach for an unusual length of time causing continued irritation, possible delayed intoxication, but more probably nausea, which is mercifully terminated by regurgitation.

Miscellaneous factors. Such phenomena as stress, anger and fear are presently recognized as factors which also influence the emptying of the stomach.

Distribution

The alcohol, having diffused through the capillary walls of the small blood vessels in the intestines, is now circulated to all parts of the body. The route of travel includes the portal vein, liver, inferior vena cava, right side of the heart, lungs, left side of the heart, and then distribution to the various organs via the arteries. Eventually, alcohol is distributed evenly in the body's fluids and cells, achieving a concentration proportionate to the water content of the organ or tissues in question.

Two factors are cited by Tabershaw as influencing the alcohol concentration in any one organ. These factors are the blood supply of and the water present in the organ. Organs with either a *rich* blood supply or a *high* water content will achieve a higher maximum concentration of alcohol more rapidly than those organs deficient in either or both.[2] It is unfortunate, from the standpoint of intoxication, that the brain is so abundantly enriched with blood and also has such a high content of water.

According to Greenberg, the body as a whole is estimated to be about 70 per cent water, and by analysis, the blood is approximately 90 per cent water.[3] Different body fluids, tissues and organs vary from these figures to a significant degree. In similar fashion, the alcohol content of each fluid or structure will show a corresponding variance. By calculation, then, it is possible to determine from the amount of alcohol in the blood, the quantity of alcohol which has been absorbed into the bloodstream and is present in the body. This *blood-alcohol level* is the ratio of alcohol present in the blood to the total volume of blood, expressed as a per cent. Thus, a blood-alcohol level of 0.15 per cent equals 1.5 parts of ethyl alcohol to 1,000 parts of blood.

The distribution of alcohol continues a general dilution process which began when the beverage was consumed. Not only is the alcohol diluted or made less concentrated by the nonalcoholic contents of the beverage, and the food contents of the stomach, but now the blood itself and the tissue fluid further dilute the alcohol. Regardless of the original alcohol concentration of the beverage, the blood-alcohol level rarely

---

[2]*Ibid.*, p. 145.
[3]Leon A. Greenberg, *What the Body Does With Alcohol* (New Brunswick, N. J.: Rutgers Center of Alcohol Studies, 1955), p. 8.

exceeds a concentration in excess of 0.55 per cent,[4] for example, 5.5 parts of alcohol to 1,000 parts of blood. The "moderate" drinker's blood-alcohol level approximates only a few hundredths of 1 per cent.

Oxidation

Most of the alcohol ingested and absorbed, more than 90 per cent, is eventually combined with oxygen. This process of oxidation results in the decomposition of alcohol into water and carbon dioxide and the production of heat and energy.

Oxidation of alcohol proceeds in three phases. The first involves the conversion of ethyl alcohol into acetaldehyde. This occurs in the liver where an enzyme functions as a catalyst in the chemical reaction. Immediately thereafter, acetaldehyde, a toxic substance, is oxidized to acetic acid. Such a reaction apparently takes place both within the liver and in other organs. Although authorities disagree as to the site of the third phase, acetic acid is changed into water and carbon dioxide, the process yielding about seven calories of energy per gram of alcohol.

While the rate of alcohol oxidation varies from person to person due to size of liver, enzyme activity, diseases, especially those affecting the liver, and certain drugs (antabuse retards the oxidation of acetaldehyde), the average rate of disposition is estimated to be one-third ounce of pure ethyl alcohol per hour. Expressed in terms of beverage alcohol, the rate of oxidation is estimated at two-thirds to three-fourths of an ounce of whisky, or an equivalent amount of alcoholic beverage, each hour. Moreover, this rate is fairly constant for each person and no practical way of increasing the oxidation rate significantly has been developed. *Such practices as vigorous exercising, the use of stimulant drugs, ingestion of foods, vitamins and black coffee, exposure to air, and the taking of cold showers have no accelerating effect on the rate of alcohol oxidation.*

As previously mentioned, the oxidation of alcohol yields approximately seven calories per gram. Thus, a serving of beer supplies from 145 to 215 calories, and one serving of table wine yields a calorie range between 100 to 120 calories. Both beer and wine, it should be noted, contain a considerable proportion of unfermented sugars and other carbohydrates which add to the caloric yield. Distilled spirits usually supply 100 to 125 calories per serving. *Only as a source of caloric energy can alcohol be classified as a food, since it is deficient in proteins, vitamins and minerals.*

The oxidation of alcohol is a continuous process and occurs until all the substance has been disposed. Since alcohol cannot be stored in the body, it is utilized for energy first while other foods are stored as fat or in the form of glycogen. With the prolonged, daily consumption

---

[4]Harold E. Himwich, "The Physiology of Alcohol," reprinted from *The Journal of the American Medical Association,* 163-547, 1957.

of large quantities of alcohol, two conditions are likely to result. There is either an increase in body weight, if other foods are not limited, or there is the development of certain "deficiency diseases" and other medical disorders prevalent among those who routinely drink their meals. The latter situation frequently results because the alcohol satisfies caloric needs but lacks vitamins and minerals for regulatory functions and proteins for tissue maintenance and repair.

While the body acts on and utilizes alcohol, alcohol evokes numerous reactions on the part of the drinker.

Effects on the Brain

There seems to be common agreement that the most immediate and dramatic consequences of alcohol ingestion pertain to altered feeling and conduct. Such modifications of mood and behavior are due to the action of alcohol on the central nervous system, specifically the brain, and are in direct proportion to the concentration of alcohol in the blood. Note that alcohol's effect on the brain is functional and temporary: functional because the cells are not destroyed, dissolved or corroded, but impaired in working ability; and temporary because the efficiency of cellular function is restored as alcohol is oxidized.

Because of the close agreement between the alcohol levels of the blood and the brain, the blood-alcohol level is frequently cited with respect to various predictable effects of drinking. For instance, most drinkers who have a relatively low blood-alcohol concentration (0.01 per cent to 0.03 per cent) will experience only mild effects, such as, slight changes in feeling, heightening of existing moods and minimal impairment of mental functions. As blood alcohol levels increase, the degree of mental inefficiency increases, drinkers experience increased feelings of relaxation and sedation, and control of voluntary muscles declines especially in the performance of fine motor skills. *Although there is considerable variation among drinkers with respect to blood-alcohol level and specific impairments, studies cited by Harger indicate that definite impairments begin in a "zone" ranging from 0.03 per cent to just below 0.10 per cent.*[5]

Functional impairment in most individuals progresses rapidly and more noticeably after the blood-alcohol level reaches 0.10 per cent. Such impairment, if it has not already occurred at lower blood-alcohol concentrations, takes the form of decreased inhibitions, less efficient vision and hearing, slurring of speech, difficulty in the performance of gross

[5]Rolla N. Harger, "The Response of the Body to Different Concentrations of Alcohol: Chemical Tests for Intoxication," *Alcohol Education for Classroom and Community,* ed., Raymond G. McCarthy (New York: McGraw-Hill Book Company, 1964), p. 98.

motor skills, deterioration of judgment, increased reaction time and a general feeling of euphoria. At 0.20 per cent blood-alcohol level, according to Harger as previously noted, most people display profound and manifest signs of intoxication. As the brain becomes more anesthetized, the drinker has difficulty maintaining an upright position, experiences dulled perception and minimal comprehension, and finally assumes a state of unconsciousness. If the concentration of alcohol in the blood exceeds 0.60 per cent, the drinker's brain becomes so depressed that breathing and heartbeat cease and death results. The physiological and psychological effects of alcohol are summarized in Table 2.

Alcohol, like many other biochemicals and drugs, is likely to produce a wide range of physical and mental responses. Such variance is attributed to the several factors which influence alcohol absorption, plus the individual differences associated with each drinker. *Consequently, the responses to alcohol not only vary from person to person, but can vary in the same person from day to day.* Therefore, the relationships between servings of alcoholic beverages and blood-alcohol concentrations, illustrated in Table 2, are approximate only. (The oxidation rate of 0.015 per cent per hour reduces blood-alcohol levels even while consumption and absorption continue, thus introducing another element of variability into the same relationships.) The effects of drinking, however, based on blood-alcohol levels, are definitely predictable and represent a progressive, depressent action on the brain.

This *depressant action is* one of of slowing down, dulling, blunting, or impairing brain function, both perception and motor function. While undiluted alcohol can irritate the lining of the oral cavity and gastrointestinal tract, and small doses of alcohol may have no behavioral effects, the feeling and appearance of stimulation following drinking is generally symptomatic of alcohol's numbing or anesthetic quality. The talkativeness, noiseness, excited feelings and increased activity are the results of lowered inhibitions and sedation. When normal restraints are removed, when the superego is dissolved, the drinker is inclined to do some rather unusual, even bizarre things. The sedative effect often masks body fatigue, thus promoting a sense of relief, a reduction of tension and a feeling of stimulation. The drinker's self-appraisal of his "stimulated" feelings and "improved" performance is now clouded by alcohol-induced mental impairment. Such modification of mood and behavior is only a pseudostimulation.

Authorities do not agree on the precise mechanism of brain impairment. Some state that the higher brain centers (cerebral cortex) are depressed first, followed by paralysis of the lower centers of the brain, including the medulla. More recent investigations[6] suggest that the reticular formation, a "regulatory structure," is the initial site of impairment. Alcohol affects this "master switchboard" of the brain which then

---

[6]*Alcohol and Alcoholism, op. cit.,* pp. 21-22.

TABLE 2

Relationships Among Servings of Alcoholic Beverages, Blood-Alcohol Levels and Predictable Effects on Feeling and Behavior

Servings of Alcoholic Beverages	Blood-Alcohol Levels	Effects on Feeling and Behavior
1	0.02–0.03%	Absence of overt effects; mild alteration of feelings; slight intensification of existing moods; minor impairment of judgment and memory.
2	0.05–0.06%	Feeling of warmth, relaxation, mild sedation; exaggeration of emotion and behavior; slight impairment of fine motor skills; slight increase in reaction time.
3	0.08–0.09%	Visual and hearing acuity reduced; slight speech impairment; minor disturbance of balance; increased difficulty in performing motor skills; feelings of elation or depression.
4	0.11–0.12%	Difficulty in performing many gross motor skills; uncoordinated behavior; definite impairment of mental faculties, i. e., judgment and memory, decreased inhibitions.
5	0.14–0.15%	Exhibition of major impairment of all physical and mental functions; irresponsible behavior; general feeling of euphoria; difficulty in standing, walking, talking; distorted perception and judgment.
7	0.20%	Feels confused or dazed; gross body movements cannot be made without assistance; inability to maintain an upright position.
10	0.30%	Minimum of perception and comprehension; general suspension or diminution of sensibility.
14	0.40%	Nearly complete anesthesia, absence of perception; state of unconsciousness, coma.
17	0.50%	Deep coma.
20	0.60%	Death is possible following complete anesthesia of nerve centers which control heartbeat and breathing.

alters the activity of other brain areas. Apparently, the exact nature of functional impairment is not known at the present time.

Intoxication

From a technical viewpoint, intoxication is a state of apparent malfunctioning which results from the presence of alcohol in the central nervous system. Drunkenness and inebriety are often used as synonyms of intoxication. Common slang terms which describe alcohol-induced inefficiency are plentiful, such as, *tanked, oiled, lushed, gassed, blotto, tipsy, high, plastered, tight, stoned, pie-eyed, smashed, stiff, stinko* and *crocked.* When a person consumes more alcohol than his body can oxidize in a given period of time, he most generally displays abnormal behavior patterns as indicated in Table 2. He is intoxicated.

Undoubtedly, there are varying degrees of intoxication, including "beginning impairment" and apparent or "manifest impairment." Numerous scientific investigations reveal that with a blood-alcohol level between 0.10 to 0.15 per cent, about 65 per cent of drinkers display definite signs of physical and mental impairment. Additionally, when the blood-alcohol level increases to 0.20 per cent, nearly all drinkers have difficulty walking and speaking in a normal way, and exhibit irresponsible and often antisocial behavior.

Estimating the degree of impairment by observation has proved to be very unreliable. Therefore, certain chemical tests for an objective evaluation of intoxication have been developed. They involve the determination of alcohol levels in blood, urine and the breath. The tests which are based on the constant proportion between alcohol concentrations in blood and the breath are conducted by several instruments, namely, the alcometer, drunkometer, intoximeter and breathalyzer. The medicolegal interpretations of blood-alcohol levels (results of urine and breath analysis translated into corresponding blood-alcohol concentrations) are important in determining impairment of driving ability.

Any discussion of intoxication would not be adequate if the psychological makeup of the drinker was not mentioned. Greenberg, commenting on the role of the drinker's temperament in producing behavioral reactions, recalls the words of O. Henry who once said certain individuals are "half drunk when they are sober."[7] Thus, the mood or "mindset" of the drinker will likely influence the pattern of responses. *A person who drinks with the expectation of getting "high" will often display "psychological intoxication" before "physiological intoxication" is possible.*

The author recalls an incident in which a nonalcoholic fruit drink was served to several persons at a party. Before the beverage was served,

---

[7]Leon A. Greenberg, "Physiological Effects: Alcohol in the Body," *Drinking and Intoxication: Selected Readings in Social Attitudes and Controls,* ed., Raymond G. McCarthy (New Haven: College and University Press, 1959), p. 12.

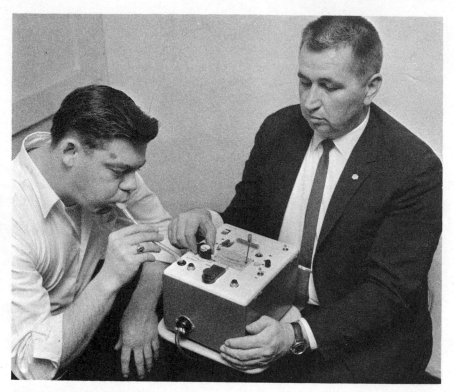

Figure 8. The Breathalyzer, a portable instrument used for determining the alcohol content of the blood by a simple "breath test." Accuracy is attained by the constant relationship that exists between the concentration of alcohol in the breath and that in the blood. (Reprinted with permission of the Stephenson Corp., a Division of Bangor Punta)

the adult guests, most of whom were infrequent drinkers, were told that vodka had been added to the drink but no taste would be detected. The results were amazing! After just a few sips, persons claimed they felt warmer; a few mentioned the feeling of dizziness; the conversation became gayer; the activity level of some increased. This situation serves well to illustrate the influence of the psyche on the body.

Not only the individual's mood, but the psychological atmosphere of drinking frequently sets the stage for certain behaviors. For instance, Todd describes the excitement which surrounds the triumph in an athletic contest as predisposing to boisterous, excessive and even bizarre behavior among youthful drinkers.[8] (Witness baseball and football championship celebrations.) The same individuals consuming the same amount of beverage alcohol in a more controlled, restrained setting will probably

---

[8]Todd, *op. cit.*, pp. 13-14.

behave in a more normal, mature way. Since the atmosphere does not call forth or permit the peculiar actions of manifest intoxication, none are evidenced, perhaps for fear of being ostracized. Could it be that drinking serves as a convenient excuse for some to act in a carefree, careless, irresponsible manner? *Maybe all drinkers could be more discriminating with regard to the psychological setting for their consumption of alcohol.*

The psychological factor is also thought to play a major part in the case of the experienced drinker's *tolerance* to alcohol. This tolerance does not refer to the resistance of the brain to the depressant action of alcohol. Rather, tolerance is most often explained as the ability to control one's action and display normal behavior patterns in spite of an elevated blood-alcohol concentration. Such reactions are thought to be learned over an extended period of time and practice.

Other Effects of Alcohol

So far, the major focus has been on the effects of alcohol on the brain. Other body parts and body processes also can be influenced significantly.[9] Some of these responses to alcohol are listed as follows:

Liver. Studies reveal a possible temporary swelling and inflammation during severe intoxication. In cases of prolonged heavy drinking and chronic alcoholism, liver tissue often becomes shriveled and hardened with fibrous tissue, indicative of cirrhosis of the liver. This effect of alcohol is thought to be indirect. Tissue degeneration is the result of malnutrition, not damage by ethyl alcohol.

Kidneys. Increased urinary output is due to the diuretic effect of alcohol on the pituitary gland.

Cardiovascular system. Initial irritating effects in the oral cavity and upper portion of the alimentary canal result in a slight, temporary increase in heartbeat and blood pressure. Because alcohol serves to dilate the blood vessels, heat loss occurs and produces feelings of warmth and sometimes perspiration, followed by decrease in body temperature.

Stomach. Large quantities of alcohol may irritate the lining of the stomach, often resulting in long-lasting inflammation (gastritis). Increased production of gastric juices frequently occurs when beverage alcohol is ingested.

Water balance. Temporary redistribution of water in the body can occur in cases of excessive alcohol consumption. This phenomenon is not dehydration, but merely a shifting of water from within the body's cells to the intercellular spaces. No water is actually lost from the body, but the alteration of the water balance is thought to account for the

---

[9]For a detailed description of such responses, the reader should consult Mark Keller, *How Alcohol Affects the Body* (New Brunswick, N. J.: Rutgers Center of Alcohol Studies, 1955).

1. The oxidation rate of alcohol within the body is relatively constant, yet the absorption rate varies widely. Explain this phenomenon.
2. Vigorous exercise, black coffee, and ingestion of food have no accelerating effect on the rate of alcohol oxidation, yet at parties the host often serves food and coffee before "sending" people home. Does this practice have any real effect on the projected ability of the guests to drive?
3. If you were on a diet, and still wished to drink, what would you select to minimize the total caloric intake?
4. If alcohol it truly a depressant, why do businessmen use if for a 'pick up' after a hard day at the office?

sensation of thirst which follows the consumption of large amounts of beverage alcohol.

Hangover. Following the excessive intake of alcoholic beverages, many persons experience temporary yet acute distress, both physical and psychic in nature. Symptoms of the so-called hangover vary widely, but most frequently include headache, exhaustion and mental depression. Peculiarly, such symptoms tend to occur several hours after alcohol has been completely oxidized in the body. The exact nature and mechanism of the hangover remain obscure.

Numerous other effects are reported in the alcohol literature. Medical authorities tend to agree that none of these, including the ones mentioned above, have much significance with regard to the health of the drinker, as long as he remains moderate in alcohol consumption. The responses of the body to alcohol are temporary, and body functioning resumes its normal pattern after the oxidation and elimination of alcohol. Moreover, scientific interpretations of life-insurance company records suggest that the life span of moderate drinkers and abstainers does not vary.

The number one risk for most drinkers, there is no intent to minimize the tragic and disruptive nature of alcoholism, is intoxication. Not only is the intoxicated person impaired in mental and physical function, he is susceptible to the dangers of accident and exploitation. More important, perhaps, inebriety also involves a reduction in personal freedom. In comparing the inefficiency induced by alcohol with that characteristic of neuroses and psychoses, Lolli identifies three areas in which such freedom is limited. They are self-realization, self-perfection and self-determination.[10] Indeed, intoxication is a major hazard associated with the use of beverage alcohol.

---

[10]Giorgio Lolli, "Alcohol and the Family," *Community Factors in Alcohol Education,* A Report of the Second Conference on Alcohol Education, Stowe, Vermont, October 16-18, 1961 (Prepared by the Vermont Department of Education), p. 37.

CHAPTER 6

Abuse of Alcohol

Earlier, reference was made to various consequences of excessive drinking. Also, the term *problem drinking* was used to describe alcohol consumption which results in damage to the drinker, his family or his community. Problem drinkers are defined then by the results of their alcohol ingestion and have been identified as including not only those who are "addictive drinkers," the alcoholics, but those users who drive after drinking and cause accidents; those who engage in drinking in order to become intoxicated; and those who drink when such imbibing is contraindicated by a diabetic condition, an ulcer, or impaired liver function. Some problem drinkers engage in the "sport" of competitive ingestion to see which one can hold more liquor.

Personal Aspects of Problem Drinking

Evident in each case of problem drinking is an element or degree of irresponsible use, and hence, an abuse of beverage alcohol. From a personal point of view, immoderate drinking can be responsible for intoxication, death or injury by accident, loss of a job, disruption of the family, impoverishment, and deficiency and metabolic diseases often associated with excessive drinking. Dependence on alcohol as a psychological crutch to hide or mask the problems of everyday living is particularly hazardous, and especially so for the young person. *Such reliance on beverage alcohol prevents the development and practice of adequate decision-making skills so necessary in coping with the perplexing aspects and disappointments of life.*[1]

Social Aspects of Problem Drinking

The social consequences of problem drinking are equally alarming. While the relationship between alcohol and various social problems can-

[1]Todd, as previously cited, lists this aspect of alcohol use as one of the unique risks of teenage drinking.

not be explained as a direct cause-and-effect phenomenon, the results of excessive drinking are a reality. Just consider the cost to industry in terms of human resources, and the social nature of problem drinking becomes apparent. There is increased absenteeism, loss of experienced and highly trained personnel, job inefficiency, expense of recruiting and training replacements and poor relationships with fellow workers.

Family and health problems involving alcohol contribute to the exploding costs of health and welfare services. Surveys reported by Hinchliffe reveal that 10 per cent of general hospital patients have drinking problems; 15 to 20 per cent of welfare cases involve alcoholism; 30 to 40 per cent of divorce cases are associated with drinking; 60 to 80 per cent of municipal court cases are alcohol related; and 50 to 60 per cent of tuberculosis patients requiring long-term hospitalization are alcoholics.[2] Such a staggering cost is multiplied by the human suffering of deserted spouses and displaced children.

While it is not clear how much inebriety is responsible for crime or in what way, the statistics fail to mention if drinking causes criminality or if the criminals just happened to be drinking when apprehended, there is some evidence that the intoxicated person is more likely to perpetuate impulsive crimes, often against persons, than is the more temperate person. It is a cold fact, moreover, that public drunkenness accounts for much of the jail population, along with disorderly conduct and vagrancy associated with alcohol use. It is estimated that some police departments spend from one-third to one-half of their time and energies in the arrest of individuals who are publicly intoxicated.

After the arrest of these excessive drinkers, there are the added costs of jailing. In far too many cases, release is soon followed by rearrest, another sentence to jail, and then release again. The procedure is referred to as the "revolving door" routine. It is not uncommon for some alcoholics to pass through this "revolving door" at least one hundred times or more before recovery or death. Unfortunately, in the case of *Powell v. Texas*, the United States Supreme Court (June, 1968) upheld the conviction of a chronic alcoholic for public drunkenness and thereby sanctioned the "revolving door" procedure, preferring it to nonexistent alternatives for handling drunks. It would seem that confinement for required medical attention and possible rehabilitation might possibly be more just, humane and cheaper than confinement for simple drying out in jail, time and time again.

Drinking and Driving

Another social dimension of problem drinking centers on alcohol in relation to automobile safety and traffic offenses. For years, people

---

[2]*Alcoholism Outlook*, ed., J. Arthur Hinchliffe (Columbus, Ohio: The Columbus Health Department and the Columbus Area Council on Alcoholism, March, 1964), p. 2.

have been advised not to drink if they plan to drive. And for many years, people have been driving to and from drinking parties, have sustained no accidents and have disproved the sound advice, at least to their satisfaction. In most cases, they have been lucky.

Many of those who drink and then drive do not display the obvious signs of intoxication, and yet they are under the influence of alcohol. The slightly impaired judgment, the false sense of security, the slower reaction time, the narrowed peripheral vision, the double vision, the lessening of depth perception, the loss of visual acuity, the reduction of cue-taking, the inflated ego and the undue expansion of aggression all, at some time, take their toll on the highways. Many studies indicate that most drinkers are incapable of operating a motor vehicle safely after a blood-alcohol level of only 0.04 per cent. They will be able to perform the mechanical functions of operation, but not in a safe manner.

So much confusion developed around the meaning of "operating a motor vehicle under the influence of alcohol" that most authorities, upon the recommendation of the National Safety Council and the American Medical Association, have accepted the following definition originated in a 1935 decision of the Arizona Supreme Court:

> The expression "under the influence of intoxicating liquor" covers not only all the well-known and easily recognized conditions and degrees of intoxication, but any abnormal mental or physical condition which is the result of indulging in any degree in intoxicating liquors, and which tends to deprive him of that clearness of intellect and control of himself which he would otherwise possess. If the ability of the driver of an automobile has been lessened in the slightest degree by the use of intoxicating liquors, then the driver is deemed to be under the influence of intoxicating liquor. The mere fact that a driver has taken a drink does not place him under the ban of the statute unless such drink has some influence upon him, lessening in some degree his ability to handle said automobile.

Using the guidelines provided by this definition, most states have applied the following medicolegal interpretations to blood-alcohol levels for operators of motor vehicles:

1. A blood-alcohol level of 0.15 per cent or more is prima facie evidence of being under the influence of alcohol.
2. A blood alcohol-level of between 0.05 to 0.15 per cent is evidence that a person may be under the influence of alcohol (admissable, but not prima facie evidence).
3. A blood-alcohol level of 0.05 per cent or less is prima facie evidence of not being under the influence of alcohol.

During the past decade, detailed studies reported by the National Safety Council indicate that alcohol is a leading factor in at least 50 per cent of fatal auto accidents.[3] Additional investigations reveal the serious-

[3]Accident Facts (Chicago: The National Safety Council, 1966).

ness of the drinking-driving problem. They are summarized by Roalman as follows:[4]

1. Surveys of single-car fatal accidents showed that 49 per cent of the dead drivers tested had blood-alcohol concentrations of 0.15 per cent or more; 20 per cent of the dead drivers had levels between 0.05 and 0.14 per cent; and only 27 per cent had no alcohol present on testing.
2. Drivers involved in accidents are more likely to have been drinking than drivers not involved in accidents. While nearly 65 per cent of persons involved in highway accidents had at least two alcoholic drinks, 90 per cent of these drivers had three drinks and 60 per cent at least six drinks, only 5 per cent of drivers not involved in wrecks had as many as two drinks or more.
3. Alcohol is also a leading factor in the occurrence of pedestrian accidents.

In the light of such reports and other data which suggest greatly increased probability of accidents with increased blood-alcohol levels in excess of 0.04 per cent, the presumptive level of intoxication was reduced to 0.10 per cent in the Uniform Vehicle Code of 1962. However, so far, only fourteen states have adopted this revised figure.

While a variety of control measures have been developed to curb the problem of drinking and driving (enforcement of laws, more punitive measures and education of beginning drivers), none has proven as successful as the popular "implied consent law," now operable in about half of the fifty states. Such a law states that a person, upon applying for a license to operate a motor vehicle, gives his implied consent to submit to a chemical test for blood-level alcohol determination if he is suspected of driving while intoxicated. If the person refuses to submit to the test by a law enforcement officer, he loses his driving privileges.

Whether the driver under the influence of alcohol is an immoderate social drinker, an inexperienced drinker, a beginning driver or an alcoholic, he is a problem drinker and a menace not only to himself, but to others when his blood-alcohol level reaches 0.04 per cent. *For most drinkers, two or three ordinary drinks can spell disaster on the highway!*

Alcoholism: Nature

Perhaps the most extreme form of problem drinking is that of alcoholism. For many years, this condition has generated a great deal of controversy among physicians, scientists, welfare workers and the public in general. Those persons described as alcoholics have not only been controversial themselves, but have been among the most abused and neglected minority groups in terms of medical care and treatment, wel-

[4]A. R. Roalman, "Drinking and Driving: New Approaches," *Today's Health,* March, 1968, pp. 34-35.

fare and rehabilitation services, civil rights, scientific investigations and public understanding.[5]

Today, most medical authorities, behavioral scientists, legal experts and informed laymen consider alcoholism a *psychosocial, physiological disorder*. The chief characteristic of this illness is the drinker's repeated inability to control either the beginning of drinking or its termination once it has started. This concept of alcoholism as an illness has only recently enjoyed widespread acceptance. Not too long ago, alcoholism was viewed primarily as a manifestation of immorality or a basic lack of will power. There are some who still describe alcoholism as a form of self-indulgence or perverseness.

Even among "alcohologists," the term *alcoholism* is used in a variety of ways. It has been described as 1. a disease; 2. an aggregate term for alcohol-related problems; 3. problem drinking; 4. drinking in excess of ordinary dietary and social usage; 5. drinking which causes injury to the drinker's health or to his social functioning; and 6. addictive drinking. While no one definition is acceptable to all, there is a consensus that alcoholism involves *repeated, uncontrolled, compulsive* and *excessive use* of alcoholic beverages to such an extent that the individual drinker's *health* and his *interpersonal relationships are significantly impaired*. Such an interpretation of alcoholism stands in sharp distinction from the condition of intoxication, short-term inefficiency resulting from an act of free choice, as explained in an earlier chapter.

Alcoholism: Prevalence

It has been estimated that as a public health problem, alcoholism ranks as the fourth most serious concern, exceeded only by heart disease, cancer and mental illness. Furthermore, it is thought that the five million American alcoholics affect more than twenty million other persons, such as family members, employers and fellow workers. And while alcoholism is no respecter of race, color, creed, sex, ethnic group, marital status, geographical location or socio-economic status, statistics reveal some interesting facts about the prevalence of alcoholism. These are:

1. There are between four to five male alcoholics for every one female alcoholic in America today.
2. Alcoholism tends to occur most often in the age group from thirty to fifty-five.
3. The highest rates of alcoholism in America prevail in those persons from Irish and Anglo-Saxon backgrounds.
4. The lowest rates of alcoholism in America occur among Italian-Americans, Chinese-Americans and Jews, Lutherans, Episcopalians and Presbyterians.

---

[5]For an eye-opening account of the past neglect of problem drinkers, the reader should consult *Alcohol Problems:A Report to the Nation, op. cit.*, pp. 21-24.

5. Alcoholism rates tend to be higher in urban and industrialized states than in rural states.
6. Less than 4 per cent of all alcoholics are found on Skid Row, the low-rent, dilapidated section of a large city where unemployment rates are high. More than 95 per cent of alcoholics hold jobs, with the help of a sympathetic employer or a fellow worker who covers up for the alcoholic's inefficiency, and maintain homes where they are sheltered or hidden by a spouse and children.

It must be admitted that without alcohol there would be no alcoholics. However, most persons who use beverage alcohol do not develop into problem drinkers. Therefore, while alcohol is a necessary factor in alcoholism, other factors must also come into play. In fact, so many causative factors have been proposed, and so many alcoholics display such varying backgrounds and characteristics that some persons believe many alcoholisms must be prevalent rather than a single disorder.

Alcoholism: Possible Causes

Undoubtedly, the causes of alcoholism are complex and no single theory of causation has been substantiated to date. Those factors most frequently cited are discussed below:

Physical factors. The abnormal response of the alcoholic is determined by a variety of physiological factors which interfere with normal alcohol metabolism. Vitamin deficiencies, glandular malfunctions, alcohol allergies and inherited disturbances in body-chemistry equilibrium have been proposed as possible etiological factors.[6]

Psychological factors. Many authorities hold that mental and emotional factors are responsible for alcoholism. It has been observed that alcoholics generally have a low tolerance for frustration, experience unusual amounts of stress and have considerable difficulty in controlling impulses and establishing significant relationships with other persons.[7] For these reasons, it is thought that some drinkers use alcohol as a form of relief in handling various problems. Psychoanalytical theory relates alcoholism to oral frustrations or gratifications during infancy and childhood with a fixation of libidinal energy at the oral level. The possibility of faulty rearing practices is further seen as productive of states of insecurity and inferiority in the adult who turns to alcohol to reduce painful emotions.

Socio-cultural factors. While not discounting the importance of physical and psychological factors, other investigators contend that the social environment, including certain cultural influences, determines

---

[6]Mark Keller, "Alcoholism: Nature and Extent of the Problem," *The Annals of the American Academy of Political and Social Science* 315:9-10, 1958.
[7]*Alcohol Problems:A Report to the Nation, op. cit.*, pp. 45-46.

whether or not relief-drinking is learned by a drinker. According to Maxwell, relief-drinking is facilitated when the cultural or ethnic group approves of relief-drinking, and rewards heavy drinking as symbolic of group solidarity or manliness.[8] Alcoholism rates are also higher among those groups in which attitudes, practices and sanctions pertaining to alcohol use display much ambivalence. In contrast with this situation, ". . . the rate of alcoholism is low in those groups in which the drinking customs, values and sanctions are well-established, known to and agreed upon by all, and consistent with the rest of the culture."[9]

Alcoholism: Signs and Symptoms

Though the causes of alcoholism remain obscure, the signs and symptoms of this illness are well known. There is wide variation in the drinking behavior of alcoholics, but the pattern of alcohol ingestion deviates from typical social drinking so drastically that it is indicative of abnormality. This disparity between social drinking and the behavior of alcoholics has led Bacon to assert that alcoholics do not drink; they do not use alcohol in ways which characterize "drinking," as socially defined.[10]

Some early warning signals of alcoholism are an exceedingly pleasant physiological or psychological response to alcohol; the need for increased intake to produce the same effect; and the experience of alcohol-induced amnesia, the so-called blackout. The alcoholic not only begins to drink more, he drinks more often and tends to display more freedom of action than is considered appropriate for the drinking situation.

Eventually, the alcoholic needs to drink before he can cope with certain social situations. He drinks before he goes to a party; he becomes preoccupied with procuring a source of alcohol; he begins to drink alone. His intake increases rapidly because he guzzles his drinks. And then, the drinker is unable to abstain. He cannot control his drinking even though the headache and hangover would be sufficient to make a normal drinker quit. A physiological need for alcohol now exists. He craves it!

There now follows a period of identifiable physical, mental and social changes which occur in the alcohol addict. Keaton specifies these changes as nervous and gastrointestinal disorders, cirrhosis of the liver, malnutrition, the overuse of defense mechanisms in justifying drinking and intoxication, development of guilt feelings about drinking practices and a general deterioration of normal, social relationships in the home

---

[8]Milton A. Maxwell, "A Multiple Linkage Conceptualization of Alcoholism," An Exhibit to Accompany a Lecture Entitled, "The Fellowship of Alcoholics Anonymous," (New Brunswick, N. J.: Rutgers Summer School of Alcohol Studies, July 15, 1964). Mimeographed.

[9]*Alcohol and Alcoholism, op. cit.*, p. 27.

[10]Bacon, *op. cit.*

and on the job, if the alcoholic can still maintain one.[11] Chain drinking and extended "benders" are also characteristic of this period.

After a number of years, the alcoholic reaches a point at which he drinks to live and lives to drink. His entire life is now oriented around alcohol. Common aspects of this advanced phase of alcoholism are also cited by Keaton. They include a complete ethical breakdown, unreasonable fears, delirium tremens, partial loss of motor coordination and the phenomenon of decreased tolerance, for example, decreased amounts of alcohol produce intoxication. The medical complications of alcoholism are now so severe that either institutionalization or death occurs unless there is some form of intervention.

It is worth noting that not every alcoholic experiences all the foregoing signs and symptoms. Moreover, the order in which the abnormal behaviors occur displays great variation. These phenomena have led many to believe that more than one type of alcoholism exists. The late E. M. Jellinek classified several types of alcoholism which are interpreted briefly as follows:[12]

1. *Alpha alcoholism,* an entirely psychological reliance on alcohol to relieve physical and psychic pain. There is *no* loss of control or inability to abstain.

2. *Beta alcoholism,* a type of of alcoholism in which severe medical complications occur, such as nerve irritations, gastric disturbances and cirrhosis of the liver. There is neither physical nor psychological dependence. No withdrawal symptoms are manifest.

3. *Gamma alcoholism,* the most prevalent form of alcoholism seen in America. It is characterized by psychological dependence, physical dependence, tissue tolerance, loss of control and withdrawal symptoms.

4. *Delta alcoholism,* the predominant form of alcoholism in France. It is similar to the gamma type except that instead of loss of control, there is inability to abstain.

5. Lesser types of alcoholism are identified as periodic, explosive, week-end and fiesta drinking.

Alcoholism: Addiction

Throughout the literature on alcoholism, several terms and processes which pertain to the addictive state are frequently employed. A brief explanation of these is most pertinent to an understanding of the widely held *theory* of alcohol addiction.

Psychological dependence, the reliance on alcohol to relieve psychic or physical distress. The drinker finds courage, strength, relief and

---

[11]William L. Keaton, *Understanding Alcoholism* (Lansing: Alcoholism Program, Michigan Department of Public Health, 1966).

[12]E. M. Jellinek, *The Disease Concept of Alcoholism* (New Brunswick, N. J.: Hillhouse Press, 1960), pp. 35-38.

identity through alcohol. Before he makes an important decision, he prepares himself with a couple of drinks.

Physiological tolerance (tissue tolerance), the condition of an alcoholic in which increasingly larger amounts of alcohol are required in order to produce an effect of well-being formerly obtained by smaller doses. This is probably the result of adaptive cell metabolism. Apparently, there are individual limits beyond which any elevation of blood-alcohol level will render such an alcoholic physically incapable of additional consumption.

Physiological dependence (physical need), the condition in which the protoplasm of brain cells, having adapted to the frequent introduction of alcohol, require the presence of alcohol in order to function.

Withdrawal symptoms, the physical and psychological effects which the alcoholic experiences when his intake of alcohol is suddenly stopped. These effects include involuntary shaking of the body or convulsion, restlessness, mental confusion and hallucinations of a terrifying nature, all collectively referred to as delirium tremens.

There are, however, many scientists, medical experts and alcohol specialists who are unable to equate alcohol addiction with narcotics addiction. In fact, the World Health Organization has considered the pharmacological action of alcohol as intermediate between habit-forming drugs and addiction-producing drugs.[13] It must be recognized that there are significant differences between alcohol and the narcotics with respect to numbers of users who become addicted, amounts required to produce addiction and length of time required for the occurrence of addiction.

To skirt some of the missing links and complications of the addiction theory,[14] the more recent term, *alcohol dependence,* has been employed in the alcoholism vocabulary. *Alcohol dependence* is a collective term which describes the consumption of alcohol in excess of cultural limits, in inappropriate places and at inappropriate times, and in such a manner as to result in harm to the drinker or to society.

Alcoholism: Treatment and Rehabilitation

From all the available evidence, there are no cures for alcoholism in the sense of antibiotics, surgical procedures or radiation therapy. (The expectation of ever resuming moderate, social drinking is held as practically impossible by most experts.) The numerous possible causes and predispositions and the diversity of alcoholic behavior patterns suggest

---

[13]*Drinking and Intoxication: Selected Readings in Social Attitudes and Controls,* ed., Raymond G. McCarthy (New Haven: College and University Press, 1959), p. 26.

[14]For a provocative interpretation of the addictive nature of alcoholism, the reader is referred to Kenneth N. Anderson, "No Hiding Place in a Bottle," *Today's Health,* March, 1965, pp. 33, 72-75.

that treatments and rehabilitation would be at least as numerous and diverse. And that is precisely the case.

The general aim of "recovery procedures" is to arrest the progress of alcoholism and to help the alcoholic lead a healthy life without alcohol. However, the chances of recovery will depend on the mental and physical status and the motivation of the alcoholic at the time of intervention, and the degree of recovery desired, for example, complete, permanent abstinence or continuing abstinence fragmented on occasions by problem drinking. When all the factors involved in restoration of alcoholics are favorable, success is usually achieved in a majority of cases. Many thousands of alcoholics are helped each year.

Modern therapy for alcoholism includes the following procedures which are not listed in any particular order and which are often employed in various combinations. Note particularly the physical, psychological and sociological dimensions of alcoholism therapy.

Figure 9. Under competent supervision, group therapy provides the alcoholic an opportunity to look at, listen to, and talk with others like himself. (Reprinted with permission of the State of Florida Alcoholic Rehabilitation Program)

Recovery from the effects of withdrawal symptoms, so often present in the "drying out" process, can be facilitated by certain drugs, especially the minor tranquilizers. After detoxification has been completed, the calming effects of reserpine and chlorpromazine are once again used to promote tension reduction in the patient, thereby lessening his psychological dependence on alcohol.

Because so many chronic alcoholics are severely malnourished, attention must be given to adequate and well-balanced diets. It is commonly held that many of the diseases accompanying alcoholism are manifestations of malnutrition. These include cirrhosis of the liver, described earlier, and various disorders of the nervous system, namely, polyneuritis, Warnicke's syndrome and Korsakoff's psychosis. Faulty nutrition is also thought to be a factor in the prevalence of active tuberculosis in alcoholics. Of course, these specific disease entities would require specific medical therapies.

After medical treatment of infections and diseases has begun, physicians sometimes employ aversion therapy in which chemical agents, electric shock and hypnotic suggestion are used to create a violent and unpleasant association with alcohol. Antabuse and certain emetics are commonly used to produce the desired, conditioned response of nausea, vomiting, piercing headaches, rapid heartbeat, flushing and hyperventilation whenever alcohol is ingested.

In psychotherapy, the purposeful conversation between a trained counselor and his client (patient), there is an attempt to help the alcoholic ". . . change his feelings, attitudes and behavior in order to live more effectively."[15] Such a process involves intense self-analysis and self-acceptance, which in some experimental settings have been promoted by the use of lysergic acid diethylamide. Other forms of psychotherapy which also seek to reveal basic tensions and hidden fears are the self-expressive psychodrama and group therapy with its feature of mutual support.

One of the more successful and publicized approaches in recovery from alcoholism is Alcoholics Anonymous, a fellowship of problem drinkers who want help in maintaining sobriety. Voluntary membership involves an emotional commitment that the alcoholic is powerless over the control of alcohol and a recognition that only a power greater than one's-self can restore soundness of mind. AA's quasireligious program of mutual understanding and assistance is based on the famous twelve steps. Patterned closely after Alcoholics Anonymous are the Al-Anon Family Groups for spouses of recovered and recovering alcoholics, and Alateen groups for the children of AA members.

The therapies described above could be offered through many individuals and groups and in a variety of facilities. There are private physicians; alcohol information centers; pastoral counseling programs of

---

[15]*Alcohol and Alcoholism, opt. cit.*, p. 33.

TWELVE STEPS OF ALCOHOLICS ANONYMOUS

1—We admitted we were powerless over alcohol—that our lives had become unmanageable.

2—Came to believe that a Power greater than ourselves could restore us to sanity.

3—Made a decision to turn our will and our lives over to the care of God *as we understood Him.*

4—Made a searching and fearless moral inventory of ourselves.

5—Admitted to God, to ourselves and to another human being the exact nature of our wrongs.

6—Were entirely ready to have God remove all these defects of character.

7—Humbly asked Him to remove our shortcomings.

8—Made a list of all persons we had harmed, and became willing to make amends to them all.

9—Made direct amends to such people wherever possible, except when to do so would injure them or others.

10—Continued to take personal inventory and when we were wrong promptly admitted it.

11—Sought through prayer and meditation to improve our conscious contact with God, *as we understood Him,* praying only for knowledge of His will for us and the power to carry that out.

12—Having had a spiritual awakening as the result of these steps, we tried to carry this message to alcoholics, and to practice these principles in all our affairs.

Figure 10. The Twelve Steps describe the philosophy and program of Alcoholics Anonymous. (Reprinted with permission of Alcoholics Anonymous World Services, Inc.)

some churches; general hospitals offering emergency services, inpatient care and outpatient care through alcoholism clinics; mental hospitals providing residential care; and halfway houses, where recovered alcoholics receive semicustodial care while adjusting to independent living following institutionalization. Far too often, the demand for these services exceeds the supply, and the facilities are overcrowded or nonexistent.

For a nation which prides itself in rehabilitation services and health care facilities and in helping those in need, it is a true paradox when vast numbers of problem drinkers wind up in jail or in prison. Instead of tried and proven therapies, they are offered the "revolving door." Some progress in the care and treatment of alcoholics is being made; some attention is at last being given to the prevention of alcoholism through education, but until alcoholism is perceived as a public health problem, such progress is bound to be slow.

SELECTED REFERENCES

ANDERSON, KENNETH N., "No Hiding Place in a Bottle," *Today's Health*, March, 1965, 33, 72-75.

BACON, SELDEN D., ed., "Studies of Driving and Drinking," *Quarterly Journal of Studies on Alcohol*, Supplement, No. 4, New Brunswick, N. J.: Rutgers Center of Alcohol Studies, May, 1968.

———, ed., "Understanding Alcoholism," *The Annals of the American Academy of Political and Social Science* CCCXV, January, 1958.

BLAKESLEE, ALTON L., *Alcoholism: A Sickness That Can Be Beaten*, New York: Public Affairs Committee, 1964.

CAIN, ARTHUR H., *Young People and Drinking*, New York: The John Day Company, 1963.

Children's Bureau and National Institute of Mental Health, *Thinking About Drinking*, U. S. Government Printing Office, 1968.

Cooperative Commission on the Study of Alcoholism, *Alcohol Problems: A Report to the Nation*, A Study Prepared by Thomas F. A. Plaut, New York: Oxford University Press, 1967.

GREENBERG, LEON A., *What the Body Does with Alcohol*, New Brunswick, N. J.: Rutgers Center of Alcohol Studies, 1955.

HOFF, EBBE CURTIS, *Decisions About Alcohol*, New York: The Seabury Press, 1961.

JELLINEK, E. M., *The Disease Concept of Alcoholism*, New Brunswick, N. J.: Hillhouse Press, 1960.

KELLER, MARK, *How Alcohol Affects the Body*, New Brunswick, N. J.: Rutgers Center of Alcohol Studies, 1955.

McCARTHY, RAYMOND G., *Community Opinions on Alcohol Problems: A Discussion Guide for Questions About Alcohol*, New Brunswick, N. J.: Rutgers Center of Alcohol Studies, 1956.

———, *Individual Attitudes: A Discussion Guide for Questions About Alcohol*, New Brunswick, N. J.: Rutgers Center of Alcohol Studies, 1956.

———, *Physiological Effects: A Discussion Guide for Questions About Alcohol*, New Brunswick, N. J.: Rutgers Center of Alcohol Studies, 1956.

———, ed., *Drinking and Intoxication*, New Haven, Conn.: College and University Press, 1959.

1. What is meant by the 'revolving door' concept?
2. Some students claim that they are better drivers after drinking moderate amounts of alcohol. Could this be possible? Explain.
3. Consider the "implied consent law" now operable in about half of the fifty states—is it a violation of the Constitution? Would you abide by it in all cases?
4. Compare the terms "intoxication" and "alcoholism".
5. What types of alcoholism might be more prevalent among students?

———, ed., *Alcohol Education for Classroom and Community,* New York: McGraw-Hill Book Company, 1964.

———, *Facts About Alcohol,* rev. by John J. Pasciutti, Chicago: Science Research Associates, Inc., 1967.

PITTMAN, DAVID J. and CHARLES R. SNYDER, ed., *Society, Culture, and Drinking Patterns,* New York: John Wiley & Sons, Inc., 1962.

ROALMAN, A. R., "Drinking and Driving: New Approaches," *Today's Health,* March, 1968, pp. 33-35, 74-75.

TODD, FRANCES, *Teaching About Alcohol,* New York: McGraw-Hill Book Company, 1964.

National Center for Prevention and Control of Alcoholism, National Institute of Mental Health, *Alcohol and Alcoholism,* U. S. Government Printing Office, 1967.

UNTERBERGER, HILMA and LENA DiCICCO, "Alcohol Education Re-Evaluated," *The Bulletin of the National Association of Secondary School Principals,* 52:15-29, 1968.

Index